AltStrings Fiddle Method

FOR BASS

Book 1

Orchestra

Second Edition

Caroline McCaskey

Music Arranged by Caroline McCaskey

Cover Design: Mary Margaret McMurtry
www.marymcmurtrydesign.com

Cover Art and Illustrations: Jessica Blackburn, Blackburn Renderings
www.blackburnrenderings.com

Graphic Layout and Music Engraving: Charylu Roberts, O.Ruby Productions
www.selfpublishmusicbooks.com

ISBN 978-1-952077-09-8

Table of Contents

Songs

For additional multimedia content including video lessons on each tune and technique, point the camera on your mobile device at the QR codes found throughout the book, or follow the links to *altstrings.com*.

Thank You for Choosing the AltStrings Fiddle Method!

There are two purposes to this series:

1. To provide the student with an introduction to playing North American and Celtic instrumental folk music, including adding ornamentation, playing backup chords and rhythms, and creating twin fiddle parts and other harmonies. This book can be used on its own, or as a supplement to classical study.

2. To offer a pedagogically appropriate resource for supplemental study to any of the mainstream teaching methods, aiming to be useful to both students and teachers regardless of prior experience or training in playing traditional music. My hope is that this method is helpful to both teachers and students, whether they have a strong traditional music background or are just beginning their non-classical journey.

	TUNE	KEY	SKILLS
1.	Twinkle, Twinkle Little Star	D	"Down Little Up little" bowing
2.	Mary Had a Little Lamb	D	Scale motion, "tunnel" fourth finger over G string
3.	Goodbye Liza Jane	D	Scale motion and rapid string crossings
4.	Highland Laddie	D	Introduces A string
5.	Kerry Polka	G	Rapid string crossings with many open strings
6.	Cripple Creek	D	Can be used to teach or reinforce D Major arpeggio
7.	Rubber Dolly	D	Long notes (opportunity to save bow), significant A string usage
8.	Moneymusk	D	Steady eighth notes, four-note patterns
9.	Old Joe Clark	D mix	Introduces C natural
10.	Peek-A-Boo Waltz	G	Longer melody, use of C natural
11.	Cluck Old Hen	D mix/d min	Introduces slides, to both F sharp and F natural
12.	Skye Boat Song	G	Introduces hooked bowing and slurs
13.	La Bastringue	G	F sharp vs. F natural, arpeggiation
14.	Soldier's Joy	G	Reinforces G Major arpeggio, introduces E string
15.	Sweet Betsy from Pike	C	Can be used to teach or reinforce C Major arpeggio
16.	Love Somebody	G	Hooked bowing (up bows on two repeated notes)
17.	Red Haired Boy	D mix	Slurring groups of two eighth notes
18.	Row Your Boat	D	Hooked bowing (down bows and up bows)
19.	Pop Goes the Weasel	C	Hooked bowing, left hand pizzicato
20.	Off She Goes	G	Complex rhythm / bowing

Posture

How to Hold the Double Bass (By Kim Bird)

Standing

Hold the bass at the bottom of the neck with your left arm off to your side. Adjust the end pin on your bass so that it is just tall enough for your arm to be raised to your shoulder when holding the neck.

Take a few steps towards the bass, and let it rest against you. You should feel the corners of the bass on your stomach and right leg. Practice letting the bass rest against you without holding it with your hands. Keep your feet shoulder-width apart, evenly balanced and avoid locking your knees. Being able to balance the bass with your body means you can use your hands to play the instrument, not to hold it.

Raise your left arm as if picking up a glass of water, keeping your shoulders relaxed, and grasp the neck. Now imagine you are holding a tennis ball instead of a bass neck with your fingers curved in a strong "C" shape.

Place your left hand thumbprint on the middle of the neck, and imagine your thumb making contact with your middle finger through the fingerboard. There should be some space between the palm of your hand and the instrument. Use the weight of your arm, not your fingers, to hold down the strings.

Do not rest your left elbow on the instrument. Your shoulders and arms should always feel open and relaxed, as if giving the bass a hug.

How to Hold the Bow

German Bow

Imagine wrapping your right hand around a water glass. Drop the frog of the bow into your hand so that it rests between your thumb and pointer finger. Place your thumb on the top of the stick, with the tip of your pinky supporting the bottom of the frog. Practice holding the bow with just your thumb and pinky for a bit. Now place your pointer and middle finger on the side of the stick to meet your thumb and let your ring finger rest on the inside curve of the frog. Try to always keep your fingers curved and keep a little pocket of air around the frog.

Putting it All Together

Practice holding the bow out in front of you, keeping it parallel to the ground. Once you can balance the bow like this, lower your arm so the bow rests on the strings. Keep your right elbow relaxed, not locked or straight.

Check your bow in a mirror to make sure it is parallel to the bridge. This is very hard to see without a mirror, so practice in front of one so you can learn what it should look and feel like.

Relax your right shoulder and use the weight of your whole arm to pull down bow the across the strings. Lead with your elbow to push up bow and return. Your elbow and shoulder should always be open and round. Check yourself in the mirror to see how you need adjust to keep the bow parallel. Practice on open strings until it feels comfortable.

How to Use Your Hands

Practice letting the bass neck rest against only your thumb on the back of the neck. Then put all four fingers on the same string and practice pushing down and releasing, keeping your fingers on the string. Keep your fingers curved with a little bit of space between them.

Don't try to squeeze the neck, let the weight of your whole hand help to push down the strings. Also, your ring finger and middle finger are a unit. Always try to maintain a hand shape that allows your index finger, middle finger and pinky to push down the strings at any time.

Pre-Flight Checklist

Just as a pilot checks his plane before takeoff, you should check your setup EVERY TIME before you play, until doing it the right way becomes the easy way.

Don't give up! It seems like a long list, but if you prepare carefully, it will quickly become muscle memory.

Here is your checklist:

General

- Feet shoulder-width apart and weight balanced evenly
- Bass rests against body

Left Hand

- Strong "C" shape with curved fingers
- Relaxed shoulder, elbow does not rest on bass

Bow Hand

- Curved fingers
- Relaxed shoulder
- Elbow does not lock

Twinkle, Twinkle Little Star

History

This popular French lullaby has been used many times as the theme for a set of variations, including by Wolfgang Amadeus Mozart and Dr. Shinichi Suzuki.

Performance Notes

Turn this tune into a duet! Play the rhythm of this tune on first finger A on the G string while a friend or your teacher plays the tune, then switch. This will make it sound like the drone strings on a fiddle!

altstrings.com/
orch-fiddle-bk1-1

Mary Had a Little Lamb

Lyrics

Mary had a little lamb,
Little lamb, little lamb,
Mary had a little lamb whose
Fleece was white as snow.

Everywhere that Mary went,
Mary went, Mary went,
Everywhere that Mary went,
The lamb was sure to go.

History

Originally from England, this song is now sung by children in English-speaking countries around the world.

Performance Notes

Try to leave your fourth finger down on the D string while you play A in bar 4; you'll need it again in bar 5!

altstrings.com/
orch-fiddle-bk1-2

Goodbye Liza Jane

Lyrics

1. Swing your Ma, swing your Pa,
   Goodbye, goodbye,
   Swing the girl from Arkansas,
   Goodbye Liza Jane.

2. Oh, how I loved her,
   Ain't that a shame?
   Oh, how I loved her,
   Goodbye Liza Jane.

History

A version of this song was collected by an African-American song collector named Thomas Talley in 1922.

Performance Notes

Try to leave your first finger down in bars 9 and 10, as you'll need it again several times. Do the same thing in bars 13 and 14. This is good bass technique!

altstrings.com/
orch-fiddle-bk1-3

9

Highland Laddie

History

This march has been used by Commonwealth military forces since the 1880s, and is still used by some regiments today. The tune also has a specific dance that goes along with it, as well as several sets of lyrics.

Performance Notes

This is our first tune that includes the A string. You can lower your bow arm and elbow to tip your bow to the A string. You can also bring your left elbow forward to help your fingers reach the A string, but be sure not to raise your left shoulder. Don't forget to drop your elbow again for the D and G strings.

This is good bass technique!

altstrings.com/
orch-fiddle-bk1-4

Kerry Polka

History

A polka is a type of dance from Bohemia, which is now part of the Czech Republic. The polka was introduced to Ireland in the late 19th century. Today there are hundreds of Irish polkas, which are played on the fiddle or button accordion.

Performance Notes

If you aren't shifting yet, that's okay! In bars 9 and 13, the high D can be played as an open D string instead.

altstrings.com/
orch-fiddle-bk1-5

Cripple Creek

Lyrics

Goin' up to Cripple Creek, goin' on a run,
Goin' up to Cripple Creek to have a little fun.
Goin' up to Cripple Creek, goin' on a whirl,
Goin' up to Cripple Creek to see my girl.

History

This is a folk song from the Appalachian Mountains. The name "Cripple Creek" might either refer to a place in Virginia, or Colorado during the Gold Rush.

Performance Notes

Walking Fingers: When this tune gets to the fourth finger, try placing only your third and fourth fingers on the D string at the beginning. This will make it faster to pick up to play the G string. Wrists like to bend when the fourth finger goes down, so make sure your wrist stays straight! Then, in bar 1 after the G string, try leaving your first finger down while you place your fourth on D, and pick it up only once your fourth finger is down. Continue to leave your old finger down as if your fingers are "walking." This may be tricky at first, but once you can do it, it's a lot faster! Try "walking" from one finger to another in this tune—you ought to be able to do it with every note except when the open strings interrupt you. See how far you can get!

Check out *AltStrings.com* for a video lesson on this technique!

Let's Duet!

Chords symbols are letters (and sometimes other symbols), which are short-hand for a collection of several notes. Let's start with one note at a time—the "root." When you see the letter "A" you can play your open A string, for "D" you can play your D string, and for "G" you can play your G string.

altstrings.com/
orch-fiddle-bk1-6

In the blank spaces, write the previous chord again (and in some cases, again and again), until you reach the next chord. For example, fill in the first blank with a "D."

Ask a friend or your teacher to play the tune, or listen to the recording, while you:

1. Trace your finger along with the music, and say the letter of the chord on each beat.
2. Play one of your open strings on each beat. If the chord symbol says "D," play your D string, etc.

Time Machine

Let's go back in time, and add chords to a one of your review tunes. Be sure to check out *AltStrings.com* for help, and practice playing along with the video lessons.

Now that you can play from a chord chart, you can play the tunes you know as duets with your friends!

Goodbye Liza Jane

Rubber Dolly

J. B. Lampe, 1869–1929

Lyrics

My momma told me, if I was goody,
That she would buy me a rubber dolly.
But don't you tell her I got a feller,
'Cuz she won't buy me a rubber dolly.

History

This children's song was once used as a playground song for hand clapping games.

Performance Notes

This is a great tune to practice walking fingers! Every time you have notes going in a down direction without skipping any notes (you can call this a descending scale), you can use walking fingers.

In bar 3, when switching from the A string to the D string, be sure and drop your left elbow at the same time so that you keep a good hand position on each string.

altstrings.com/
orch-fiddle-bk1-7

Moneymusk

History

Moneymusk is the name of a town in Scotland. This tune is usually played as a strathspey, a type of tune unique to Scotland. Here, it is arranged as a reel.

Performance Notes

1. Try to stay in the middle of the bow.

2. Open and close your arm to keep the bow straight.

3. To play faster, try using less bow.

Backup Chords

Go back through this tune and write in chords so that there are two chords per bar. The chords should look like this:

$\frac{4}{4}$ D D | D G | D D | G A :‖

‖: D D | D D | D D | G A :‖

altstrings.com/
orch-fiddle-bk1-8

15

Ghost/Accent: "Little BIG and" Pattern

Try this in the air first without the bow, or by "soaping" on your arm (Imagine you have soap on your bow hand, and use up and down bow strokes to pretend to scrub your left arm). Once it is easy to do that correctly, go ahead and try it on your D string, and then on any other strings you'd like to try. Remember to keep your wrist and fingers loose! The pattern should go like this:

Lit - tle BIG and

Notes

1. Any accented note should be played with greater bow speed, arm weight and "bite" in the bow hand than the other notes.

2. Any non-accented note should be played with very little bow speed and zero arm weight, and should barely be heard at all. This type of playing is called "ghosting" the bow, and can be used to count with your bow, enabling placement of even very complicated accent patterns.

3. A non-accented note immediately following an accented note can be played with greater bow speed than the other ghosted notes, in order to make up for the amount of bow you used to play your accent. The note should still be played with no arm weight so as not to sound like an accented note.

Once you can do the "Little BIG and" pattern on your open strings, try using it once per chord in our chord progression for "Moneymusk" (there should be two patterns per bar).

Try it as a duet! It should go like this:

Another option is to add your first finger to the G string instead of using open A; this will eliminate the fast string crossings.

Old Joe Clark

Lyrics

Old Joe Clark he had a house,
Fifteen stories high,
Every story in that house was
Filled with chicken pie.

Fare ye well, Old Joe Clark,
Fare ye well I say,
Fare ye well, Old Joe Clark,
I'm a-goin' away.

History

Originally a ballad about a mountaineer, this song has ninety verses!

Performance Notes

This tune uses a second finger on the A string (C natural), and a fourth finger on the D string (F sharp).

altstrings.com/
orch-fiddle-bk1-9

Peek-A-Boo Waltz

William J. Scanlan, 1856–1898

Lyrics

Peek-a-boo, peek-a-boo,
Come from behind the chair;
Peek-a-boo, peek-a-boo,
I see you hiding there.

History

This fiddle tune was originally a song, and the verse (A part) was in duple meter and the chorus (B part) was in waltz time. Today, the whole tune is played as a waltz.

Performance Notes

This tune is full of half notes! Save your bow on the half notes, and also make sure to hold each half note for two beats. That way, people can dance to it!

altstrings.com/
orch-fiddle-bk1-10

Cluck Old Hen

Lyrics

My old hen's a good old hen,
She lays eggs for the railroad men.
Sometimes one, sometimes two,
That's enough for the whole darn crew.

Cluck old hen, cluck and sing,
Ain't laid an egg since way last spring.
Cluck old hen, cluck and squall,
Ain't laid an egg since way last fall.

History

The oldest version of this very old Appalachian song dates back to 1886!

Performance Notes

Slides: In this tune, try sliding your second or fourth fingers while you bow.

In the A part, you can slide your fourth finger from where your second finger goes, up to the fourth finger position.

In the B part, try putting your second finger where your first finger goes, and sliding up to the second finger position from there.

altstrings.com/
orch-fiddle-bk1-11

Skye Boat Song

Lyrics

Speed bonnie boat like a bird on the wing,
Onward! the sailors cry,
Carry the lad that's born to be king
Over the sea to Skye.

History

This Scottish "lament," or sad song, is about the boat that helped Bonnie Prince Charlie, disguised as an Irish woman, escape from the British army in Scotland to the Isle of Skye.

Performance Notes

Slurs: In bars 1 and 3, each bar gets one long down bow. It's up to your finger to change the note!

Hooked bows: In bar 2, those notes are hooked bows, but since they have lines, separate the notes with more gentle strokes than you would if they had staccato dots.

Form: The *form*, or shape, of this tune is AABBA.

altstrings.com/
orch-fiddle-bk1-12

La Bastringue

History

This French Canadian fiddle tune has a specific dance that goes along with it. "La Bastringue" means "the wild party" in French.

Performance Notes

This tune uses both sharps and naturals. On the G string in this tune we always use C♮, and on the D string, sometimes it is F♯ and sometimes it is F♮. Look for the natural sign to tell you to use a second finger.

altstrings.com/
orch-fiddle-bk1-13

La Bastringue Harmony – Advanced

21

Soldier's Joy

History

This fiddle tune originates from the British Isles, and is now played around the world.

Performance Notes

This tune is played by many different styles of player, from bluegrass to Irish and many more. Try going to a "session" (an informal group of people playing traditional music) and if they ask if you'd like to play a tune, try this one! It is very likely that someone else will know it too, and you can play together. Make sure to tell them that you can play it in the key of "G." (This tune is normally played in the key of D.) Like many of the tunes in this book, it has been transposed to be easier to play for instruments without an E string.

*altstrings.com/
orch-fiddle-bk1-14*

Sweet Betsy from Pike

Lyrics

Did you ever hear tell of Sweet Betsy from Pike,
Who crossed the wide mountains with her lover Ike,
With two yoke of cattle, an old yeller dog,
A tall Shanghai rooster and a one-spotted hog?
Singing too-ra-li, oo-ra-li, oo-ra-li-ay.

History

This Gold Rush era folk song by John A. Stone is about a pioneer woman named Betsy, who migrated from Pike County (probably in Missouri) to California.

Performance Notes

Bowing: In many of our previous tunes, every bar has started with a downbow. This is because a down bow works with gravity to create an emphasis on a note, and we want to place emphasis on the first beat of the bar. If this didn't occur naturally in the tune, we added slurs or bow retakes to correct it.

Since this tune is in 3/4, we are not going to emphasize on the downbeat of every bar. Instead, we are bowing "as it comes," or alternating down and up strokes, and relying on playing with long, smooth strokes to create a longer phrase. Work with your teacher to figure out which notes could be the most important, and emphasize those notes instead. You can do this by using a little bit more bow (moving the bow faster to cover more ground with it) and sinking your arm into the string to give the bow more of the weight from your arm. Try it!

*altstrings.com/
orch-fiddle-bk1-15*

23

Love Somebody 16

History

This Irish fiddle tune goes by many other names, including "Tripping on the Mountain," "Hair in the Butter" and "Twin Sisters."

Performance Notes

The double up bows that occur throughout the tune will help you to keep a down bow on the first beat in every bar.

altstrings.com/
orch-fiddle-bk1-16

Red Haired Boy

History

This tune was originally from Ireland, and went by many other names such as "The Little Beggar Man" and "The Little Red Fox." It is now played throughout Scotland, Ireland, and North America.

Performance Notes

This is a great tune to practice your slurs! Two notes that are slurred together can be practiced first by stopping the bow in between the notes. Then, try playing the notes with the same bow direction without stopping the bow.

Please note that in this tune, we will use second finger on the A string and third finger on the D string.

altstrings.com/
orch-fiddle-bk1-17

Chords

We can already play the "root" of the chord (which is the same as the chord's name). This time, the other instruments of the orchestra will be adding the "fifth" of the chord. Since the bass plays such low notes, however, playing two notes at once (or "double stops") doesn't sound very good. We are going to continue to play only the root of the chords, and play the fifth later on in Book 2, when we learn to alternate between the two to create a rhythmic bass line.

Chopping/Vertical Bowing

Please attempt only under instructor supervision.

Let's get percussive! Chopping is a sound you can make with your bow. It doesn't sound like any particular note, because the bow moves a little bit along the string, instead of across it like normal.

The best bow hold for chopping on a bass is a French bow grip. If you are used to a German grip, ask your teacher or any friends who play the cello how to hold the bow as pictured below.

To chop, hold your bow an inch or two above the strings. Move the bow REALLY fast down onto the strings, using your arm (rather than your fingers or wrist). Let the weight of your arm sink into the string. The bow should move along the string, not in the direction of a down bow. It should make a crunching sound, and the bow should come to a complete stop in the string.

Once the bow has stopped moving, you can pick up your bow and try it again.

Be sure to stay right at the frog (where the hair is tight), but be careful not to hit the metal part of the bow on your strings or on the body of your instrument!

Once you can make a chopping sound, try to alternate it with some chord notes. Let's try "G." (Remember, we can use our G and D strings at the same time when we see "G.")

Don't pick up the bow after the chop — leave it on the string and pull the chord notes from there. Let the open strings ring as your bow is in the air getting ready to chop again. The chords are not played using a long bow, but are more like a pizzicato with your bow.

Once you can alternate ringing the strings with chopping, try it with "Soldier's Joy." (Don't worry about the D7 for now — we'll cover that in later books. Just use "D" instead.) Once you've learned "Love Somebody," you can try that one as well.

For the C chord, basses can simply play C♮ on the A string for now. Be sure to see *AltStrings.com* for video lessons on these accompaniments!

Variation: Set Chop/Soft Chop

Once the tune gets to be too fast for the Circle Chop, try this instead! Simply set your bow on the string in between chops, in rhythm, instead of playing the chord.

You can even create a variation in which you use both Circle Chop and Set Chop in one bar.

Try it, it sounds really cool!

Be sure to see *AltStrings.com* for video lessons on these accompaniments!

Here are some tunes to practice your hooked bow (two down bows or two up bows in a row).

Row Your Boat

18

* Second player starts when first
player gets here for a round.

Pop Goes the Weasel

19

Off She Goes

History

Fiddlers may have played this tune when a ship left the harbor.

Performance Notes

This tune is a great chance to practice your hooked bowing.

altstrings.com/
orch-fiddle-bk1-18

altstrings.com/
orch-fiddle-bk1-19

altstrings.com/
orch-fiddle-bk1-20

Playing in a Band

So you want to play in an existing band or put one together with your friends? Great! Here are some tips:

Usually, bands have at least one each of the following members:

- Someone whose primary job is to play the melody, and be the "face" of the ensemble
- Someone whose primary job is to play the chords
- Some type of bass player — this can be the same as the chord player

Other jobs in a band:

- Someone has to be the speaker during concerts; someone who communicates with the audience, like the narrator of the concert. This job can be passed around between band members, but usually it's primarily one person.
- Every band needs a manager, or someone to: handle booking performances, schedule and run rehearsals, and promote the band's concerts. These jobs can of course be divided among band members (or even people outside the band).

Now, on to the music!

Intros: The tune has to start somehow! Some common ways to start a tune are:

- Play "potatoes" or a count off, using the rhythm of "Twinkle, Twinkle Little Star" in *Book 1* (see the "Twinkle" lesson at *AltStrings.com* for how to add this type of introduction to a tune.)
- Play part of the tune, usually that last couple of bars, before the tune starts
- Just jump right in at the beginning of the tune!
- It works well to have one person, several people or everyone play the intro

Melody: If you know the tune, you can always play the tune! Sometimes it's nice to let one person play the tune solo with only one or two people playing the chords. If there are usually a lot of people playing the melody, this can be a nice change in sound. This is true in a jam session, too!

Chords: If you are the person playing the chords, it works well to play different rhythmic patterns over the chords each time through the tune. See the videos at *AltStrings.com* for ideas on how to accompany tunes!

Harmony: In *Book 2*, we will learn how to create harmonies using only the melody and chord symbols. It works well to play only the tune one time through, then add one or two harmony parts the second time through.

Endings: There are several ways to end a tune, and choosing different endings for different tunes makes things more interesting for the audience.

- Short stop: play the tune and simply stop short on the last note. This is a very exciting way to end a tune!
- Long ending: play the tune as normal, but extend the length of the last note.
- Variation: change the notes in the last measure or so of music to a more exciting, final-sounding ending. This is your chance to compose!
- Tag: end the tune, then add a little melody to the end (see "Twinkle, Twinkle Little Star" in *Book 1* for an example.) This is most often done in American music like Old-Time and Bluegrass.

Creating a set: Since fiddle tunes are so short, most of the time you'll want to play a tune more than once. You'll also want to play more than one tune in a row.

- When choosing tunes to play in a set together for performance, it makes the most sense to choose to use tunes that come from the same region. You may also want to put tunes of different speeds in order from slowest to fastest; for example if you're playing a Scottish set, you could play a march, then a strathspey, then reels.

- You can learn a lot by listening to how other fiddlers put their sets together..

- When arranging sets for a concert, you'll want to alternate playing fast sets with slow tunes. You usually want to start and end halves of the concert with fast tunes, and play about twice as many fast or medium-speed sets as you do slow tunes.

Tips for Jamming

- If you've been invited to lead a tune, pick one you know really well, and play it at least twice in a row so that others can join in.

- Unless you've been invited to lead a tune, it's best not to play louder than anyone else.

- It's great to try and figure out a tune by ear during a jam! That way you can learn it and join in next time you come. Be sure to ask the name of a tune you'd like to learn to make it easier to find later. You may even ask someone if you can record them playing the tune slowly for you, so that you can learn their version at home and play it with them next time.

- Before the tune starts, ask what key the tune is in. That way you can figure out which chord will be the most common. By playing the chords, you can play along with a tune you don't know.

- If someone is singing a song or playing a tune by themselves and most other people aren't playing too, it's most polite just to listen to their solo, rather than make too much noise trying to figure it out on your instrument.

- Have fun!

Check out our other books in the *AltStrings Fiddle Method* series:

Books 3 and *4* build on your exciting skills, using lots of transcriptions of real recordings by today's great fiddlers!

Continue your study of playing accompaniment with chords, creating harmonies, and adding traditional ornamentation, by seeing for yourself how the masters do it!

Our series for other instruments includes *AltStrings Fiddle Method* books for Violin, Viola and Bass.

Audio recordings and play-along backing tracks are available through iTunes, as well as at *AltStrings.com*.

Check out *AltStrings.com* for sheet music arrangements of traditional, folk, pop, rock, jazz and holiday music, for over 20 types of bowed string ensemble!

Happy Fiddling!

Acknowledgements

A big THANK YOU to the many music teachers who have shared their talent and wisdom with me over the years, especially Kathleen Spring, my Suzuki violin teacher trainer, and Bobbi Nikles, my mentor and editor, both of whom have always been so generous with their time. Thanks to my friends Kim Bird (pictured above), Evan Shelton, and Meaghan Salton, for their cello and bass expertise. Thanks to Charylu Roberts for her wonderful layout work, as well as for teaching me about the publishing industry, and being the reliable sounding board I need for all my crazy ideas. I love working with you! Thanks to Mary McMurtry and Jess Blackburn; your work is beautiful! Thanks of course to my Nicola; you are my reason. Thanks also to my family, who have by now hopefully given up on the idea that I might be a veterinarian someday.

www.ingramcontent.com/pod-product-compliance
Lightning Source LLC
LaVergne TN
LVHW081337060426
835513LV00014B/1328